THE ADVENTURES OF COWGIRL AMY!

Cowgirl Amy and the Easter Mission

A Tradition Begins

Dr. Psalm

The Adventures of Cowgirl Amy!
Cowgirl Amy and the Easter Mission by Dr Psalm
Copyright © 2015 by Peace Psalm LLC
All Rights Reserved.
ISBN: 978-1-59755-288-2

Published by: ADVANTAGE BOOKS™
　　　　　　　Longwood, Florida USA
　　　　　　　www.advbookstore.com

This book and parts thereof may not be reproduced in any form, stored in a retrieval system or transmitted in any form by any means (electronic, mechanical, photocopy, recording or otherwise) without prior written permission of the author, except as provided by United States of America copyright law.

First Printing January 2015
15 16 17 18 19 20 21 10 9 8 7 6 5 4 3 2 1
Printed in the United States of America

Cowgirl Amy and the Easter Mission

Dr. Psalm

Halo and Howdy! My name is Cowgirl Amy! I love God, my family, friends, and my pony Slow Poke! My Grandma Linda and I go on secret missions. We find God and praise in the most amazing places. Come and join us! Today Grandma Linda is calling me for some help with celebrating Easter with a new family tradition. She wears her yellow cowgirl hat when she needs my special Cowgirl Amy help.

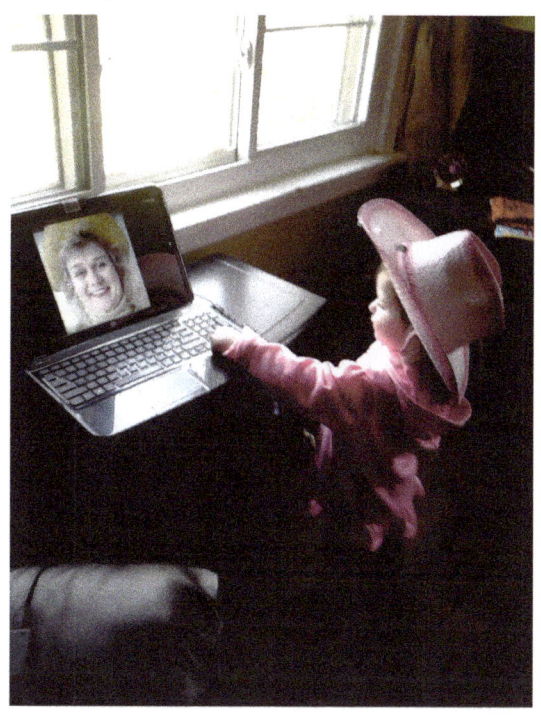

Grandma Linda called me today on Skype. She was wearing her yellow hat, so I knew she needed my help.

"Halo my Cowgirl Amy! How are you? I need your special Cowgirl Amy help!" said Grandma. "Easter is a special time when we give thanks to the Lord Jesus Christ for giving His life so we might be saved. I need your help with a family tradition that shows our thanks to Jesus and celebrates His rising. We have a week of traditions to make!" said Grandma Linda.

'All right and Yee Haw! Let's get started!" I said.

Dr. Psalm

PALM SUNDAY

Grandma Linda said "Palm Sunday is the start of Holy Week. It is called Palm Sunday, because the people waved palms leaves when Jesus entered the city of Jerusalem." She asked "How should we celebrate Palm Sunday?"

I said "I know! Let's wave palm leaves to welcome Jesus to holy week! I don't have a palm leaf, so I am going to pretend my flower book mark is a palm leaf!"

Grandma Linda said "Great ideas Cowgirl Amy!"

I said "It makes me so happy to think what it must have been like to wave to Jesus in person! Let's pray."

Thank you Heavenly Father for Your son Jesus. Thank you for the palms that we wave to say welcome to our Savior, our Lord and our King!

In the name of Jesus we pray, Amen!

Dr. Psalm
HOLY MONDAY

"Holy Monday is a day to remember that the church is for worship and praise." Grandma Linda said.

"I know! Let's go to say a prayer in a church!" I said.

"Great idea Cowgirl Amy! There is a church down the street we may go to pray." said Grandma Linda.

"Let's go! Yee haw!" I said.

Grandma said, "Cowgirl Amy, you say the prayer this time."

I said "Yee haw sure!" as I held a cross to say thank you.

Dear Jesus,
I love You, I love You, I love You!
I thank You, I thank You, I thank You!
I praise You, I praise You, I praise You!

In the name of Jesus we pray, Amen!

Dr. Psalm

HOLY TUESDAY

"On Holy Tuesday, Jesus went to Mount of Olives." said Grandma Linda.

"I know a tradition to add! An olive snack to remind us where Jesus was on Tuesday!" I said.

"Wonderful idea Cowgirl Amy! Let's pray before our snack" said Grandma Linda.

Cowgirl Amy and the Easter Mission

Dear Heavenly Father, Thank you for sending Jesus. We remember His journey to Mt Olive today. Please bless our olive snack.

In the name of Jesus we pray, Amen!

HOLY WEDNESDAY

"Holy Wednesday was another day of teaching and traveling. What do you think Cowgirl Amy?" Grandma Linda asked.

"I know! Let's wear purple and read the Bible!"

"Excellent ideas Cowgirl Amy! Purple is the color for Lent, and reading the Bible is always a great way to learn! I know just the verse to read! And, let's write it in purple!" said Grandma Linda.

"Yee haw! I have a flower book marker to mark the place in my Bible!" I said.

When the disciples asked Jesus to teach them how to pray, this is what He said:

> Our Father who art in heaven
> Hallowed be Your name
> Your kingdom come,
> Your will be done
> On earth as it is in heaven.
> Give us day by day our daily bread
> And forgive us our sins,
> For we also forgive everyone who is indebted to us.
> And do not lead us into temptation
> But deliver us from the evil one.
> For Thine is the kingdom, the power and the glory forever and ever. Amen. **(Luke 11 2-4. NKJV)**

Dr. Psalm

MAUNDAY THURSDAY

"On Thursday, Jesus had His last supper with His disciples. It is a special day." said Grandma Linda. "What do you think we should do today?" she asked.

"I know! Let's break bread and say 'Thank you Jesus' at dinner!" I said.

"Very good Cowgirl Amy!" said Grandma Linda.

Let's pray before our meal begins.

Dear Heavenly Father, thank you for giving Your only son to us. We break our bread to honor Jesus, our Lord, our Savior, our Teacher, and our King.

In the name of Jesus we pray, Amen!

Dr. Psalm

GOOD FRIDAY

"Friday is the day that Jesus died for our sins. It is a day to be thankful and humbled by His love." said Grandma Linda.

"I know! Let's be quiet for a minute, and say a thank you prayer." I said.

"Wonderful ideas Cowgirl Amy!" said Grandma Linda.

Dear Jesus, we thank You with all of our hearts. We love You in every possible way. Our minute of silence is our way to say thank you for saving us today.

In your name we pray, Amen!

HOLY SATURDAY

"Many families have Easter Egg hunts on Holy Saturday morning." said Grandma Linda.

"Yes, my mom and dad hide eggs for me to find. It is fun!" I said.

"Very good. I have a tradition to add to it. I will hide a golden egg with a surprise for Easter Sunday. Can you guess what I will put in the egg?" asked Grandma Linda.

I said. "I know! A cross to wear with my Easter outfit to church!"

Grandma Linda smiled and said "You are so right! This cross will not have Jesus on it, as it reminds us he rises and we will be with Him again someday."

"Let's pray!" I said.

Thank you Jesus for traditions so fun! Thank you for traditions to remind us You are the One!

In your name we pray, Amen!

EASTER SUNDAY

"Easter is a joyous time. It is a time to celebrate the rising of Jesus, and a reminder we will see Him again one day. I know your mom and dad will take you to church in your Easter clothes, and you will have a nice Easter lunch with family. Is there any other tradition we may add?" asked Grandma Linda.

"Yes! I want to say a thank you prayer when I wake up on Easter morning!" I said.

"That is an awesome idea Cowgirl Amy! What a wonderful way to start Easter Sunday!" said Grandma Linda.

I said "Let's pray!"

Good morning dear Jesus! Happy Easter to You! I am so happy You rose from the grave! Thank you from the top of my hat to the bottom of my toes. I love You!

In your name we pray, Amen!

Adios for now my friend! I hope you liked our new Easter Traditions! I wish a Happy Easter to you and your family!

Come and visit us next time for our Favorite Prayers for Mom Adventure! Grandma Linda and I are on a secret mission to find some favorite prayers to give thanks for my mom!

Until we meet again! Your friend, Cowgirl Amy

Dear Lord, thank you for my friends. Please watch over them and shower them with your love.

In the name of Jesus we pray, Amen!

Join Cowgirl Amy in her upcoming adventures!

- Cowgirl Amy and the Art Adventure
- Cowgirl Amy and the Texas Easter
- Cowgirl Amy and the Mystery of the Hidden Verses
- Cowgirl Amy and the Ranch at Christmas

Other adventures include:

- Cowgirl Amy and the Prayer Garden
- Cowgirl Amy and the Easter Adventure – A Tradition Begins
- Cowgirl Amy and Favorite Prayers for Mom
- Cowgirl Amy and Favorite Prayers for Dad
- Cowgirl Amy at the Cow Kid Zoo
- Cowgirl Amy and the Christmas Celebration – A Tradition Begins

SPECIAL THANKS TO:

The cross in the picture for Palm Sunday is handmade from mesquite wood by Rustic Notions. You may learn more about them on RusticNotions.com

For more information contact:

Dr Psalm
C/O Advantage Books
P.O. Box 160847
Altamonte Springs, FL 32716
info@ advbooks.com

To purchase additional copies of this book or other books published by Advantage Books call our order number at: 407-788-3110 (Book Orders Only)

or visit our bookstore website at: www.advbookstore.com

Longwood, Florida, USA
"we bring dreams to life"™
www.advbooks.com

Dr. Psalm

www.ingramcontent.com/pod-product-compliance
Lightning Source LLC
Chambersburg PA
CBHW042350040426
42449CB00018B/3480